Original title:
Woodland Wanderings

Copyright © 2025 Creative Arts Management OÜ
All rights reserved.

Author: Dorian Ashford
ISBN HARDBACK: 978-1-80567-185-5
ISBN PAPERBACK: 978-1-80567-484-9

Beneath the Bark's Embrace

A squirrel dangles from a branch,
Chasing acorns with a dance.
He trips and flips, oh what a sight,
Landing smack right on my kite!

The trees are laughing, can you hear?
Whispering secrets, oh so clear.
A woodpecker joins the fun,
Pecking beats till day is done.

Sunbeams Through the Thicket

Sunlight pours like honey gold,
Tickling leaves, so brave and bold.
A rabbit hops, it plays a game,
Ducking low, he feels no shame!

A fox prances, tail held high,
Falling flat, he gives a sigh.
His friends all giggle, what a show,
In the rays where wildflowers grow.

Where the Ferns Unfurl

Underneath the ferns so green,
A toad hops out, quite the scene.
He croaks a tune that's out of time,
A frog joins in—oh what a rhyme!

They leap and land in laughter's cheer,
Who knew such joy could thrive down here?
With every ribbit, every croak,
Melodies weave in forest smoke.

The Song of the Stream

A babbling brook, it sings away,
Telling tales of its wild play.
A fish jumps up, in a splashy flair,
A duck quacks back, "Are you up there?"

The water giggles, tickling toes,
With each ripple, the laughter flows.
It's a party here, don't miss the chance,
To join the dance in nature's prance!

Whispers of Change Through the Trees

In the forest, squirrels chatter,
While they hide their acorns and scatter.
A chipmunk slips on a wet, green leaf,
And yells out loud in comic grief.

A raccoon steals snacks from a picnic spread,
Wearing a mask, it thinks it's well-bred.
The birds sing loudly, but one sings flat,
It's a karaoke night; who invited that?

Foxes sneak peeks, oh what a sight,
Trying to dance in the pale moonlight.
But paws get tangled in old roots,
They tumble and trip in their furry suits.

The trees are swaying, in laughter's delight,
As owls hoot jokes, under stars so bright.
A bad pun echoing cheers from afar,
The night is full of giggles, bizarre!

Enchanted Shadows Whisper Along

In the forest, shadows creep,
A squirrel talks, or so I peep.
Trees giggle as the wind does sing,
A dance of branches, oh what a fling!

Beneath a thorny bush I find,
A lost shoe, very much in kind.
A rabbit grins with a cheeky wink,
I swear he's plotting—what do you think?

Mushrooms sprout with hats so grand,
While owls comment, "Isn't that bland?"
The sun slips low, casting a glow,
As shadows tangle, putting on a show.

The mossy carpet welcomes me,
A wobbly dance, come join the spree!
Each twist and turn's a giggly charm,
In this charming realm, there's no alarm.

The Journey Beyond the Fern Fronds

Past the ferns, I take a stride,
Where silly snares and goofballs hide.
A raccoon wears a striped tie,
Suggesting I should learn to fly!

The path is lined with nuts and leaves,
While chipmunks count their silly heaves.
They giggle loud, a joyful sound,
As flowers dance upon the ground.

A parrot laughs, "What brings you near?"
To which I say, "I smell the cheer!"
Pinecones drop like party confetti,
They'll tell the tales of fun and Jetty!

The winding route leads me to play,
With mushrooms that pretend to sway.
In this tangled realm of jesting souls,
My wandering heart sings countless goals!

Sun-Kissed Dreams in the Leafy Haven

In a haven where sunshine beams,
The ants plan trips in moonlit dreams.
With tiny hats and juggling acts,
Their circus greens, who knew those facts?

A bumblebee hums a tune so fine,
While fireflies blink to mark the time.
They flash their glow like starry dancers,
In the leafy shade, ignoring glancers.

The flowers giggle, their colors bright,
As I fall into a playful fright.
A deer prances with a yo-yo string,
Laughing with joy, it's quite a thing!

In this sunny, leafy space so grand,
With silly antics at each strand.
I'll dance among the buzzing cheer,
For in this haven, fun is near!

Footprints of the Forgotten Ones

Old paths whisper tales of yore,
As raccoons rummage through folklore.
Each footprint tells a different joke,
While shadows chuckle 'neath the oak.

The rusty tin can rolls to greet,
A family of ants, ready to cheat.
"Who's paying the price for yesterday?"
Their laughter echoes—what a display!

A lizard dons a trendy cap,
And struts around like he's the chap.
With every step, I'm filled with glee,
In a world where fun runs wild and free!

So let's stroll where the lost ones tread,
Their silly stories live instead.
In this patch of play, they prance and dance,
Not a worry found, just a merry chance!

Glimmers of Gold in the Green

A squirrel wore a shiny hat,
He danced around the tree like that.
The mushrooms giggled, oh what fun,
As sunlight sparkled, nearly spun.

The shadows played their silly games,
While frogs leapt high, just like their names.
The owl hooted a playful cheer,
As critters joined, no hint of fear.

A rabbit slipped in fancy shoes,
While bushes hummed their funny tunes.
They twirled and pranced, what a sight,
In the glimmers, pure delight.

So if you stroll through leafy lanes,
Just watch for laughter in the rains.
Nature's jesters, bold and bright,
Will tickle your heart with sheer delight.

Enchantments Beneath the Elder Boughs

A chipmunk told a tale so grand,
Of nuts and acorns across the land.
With twinkling eyes and toothy grin,
He jested tales where squirrels win.

The trees swayed gently, bowing low,
As birds held concerts in a show.
The bugs wore hats, their dress so smart,
Throwing a bash, a tiniest art.

An old toad croaked a croaky tune,
Dancing with shadows beneath the moon.
The crickets joined, they strummed along,
While rabbits hummed a silly song.

So take a stroll where laughter flows,
Amidst the whispers, who really knows?
Enchantments bloom beneath the boughs,
With chuckles lingering, just because.

Reflection in a Forest Pool

A frog admired his dapper face,
In the mirror-like water, what a place!
He practiced jumps and ribbits grand,
While fishes giggled, oh how they planned.

A duck waggled, with feathers askew,
"What's this reflection? Is that you?"
The turtle laughed, "Oh what a sight!
You're a fancy bird, of sheer delight!"

The water sparkled, casting jokes,
As pebbles whispered winks and pokes.
Each ripple carried laughter's tune,
In this hollow, beneath the moon.

So when you pause and share your glee,
By forest pools, just let it be.
Laughter dances in nature's thralls,
Reflecting joy, as the night calls.

An Invitation from the Undergrowth

The bushes beckoned with a laugh,
"Come play with us, we're a funny staff!"
The beetles formed a rollicking crew,
With snappy steps, they danced for you.

A hedgehog jived; his quills all spiked,
While every twig, it sat and hiked.
The flowers swayed with petals wide,
As they invited all to their ride.

The raccoons bickered over snacks,
While singing songs of clever hacks.
"Join the fun!" they chirped with glee,
In the undegrowth, wild and free.

So seize the chance, don't wait too long,
For nature knows where you belong.
Embrace the whimsy in this lush space,
And let your worries vanish without trace.

The Lure of the Leafy Labyrinth

In the maze of green, I roam,
Chasing squirrels, far from home.
They giggle as I lose my way,
A nut parade, brightens my day.

Branches wave like friendly hands,
Inviting me to make some plans.
But oh, the ticks, they come out to play,
My scalp's a buffet, hip-hip-hooray!

A rabbit hops, it takes a leap,
I join in, and now we creep.
Despite the thorns that snag my coat,
In this silliness, I gloat.

So here I skip, through muck and mire,
With silly hats, I never tire.
In leafy halls, we dance and twirl,
Nature's jesters, just unfurl.

Nature's Unwritten Poetry

A squirrel recites a little rhyme,
Flatulent frogs keep perfect time.
Nature's quirks, a play on words,
As clumsy as the nearby birds.

With acorn caps, we fashion crowns,
We waddle 'round like silly clowns.
The wind whispers secrets, they giggle bright,
Turning trees into merry sights.

I trip on roots, a comedic fall,
A raccoon chuckles, applauds it all.
Chasing butterflies, they tease and flirt,
While I roll in mud, covered in dirt.

In this wild stage where fun ensues,
Each head-scratching moment, I gladly choose.
With laughter echoing, all feel free,
Nature's jest, just you and me.

In the Heart of the Fern-Laden Glade

In the ferns, where giggles hide,
I found a toad, with froggy pride.
His croaking sounds like ancient songs,
While me, I stumble, prove him wrongs.

With mushrooms sprouting like silly hats,
We dance around like two wild brats.
Each step I take, a squeaky sound,
As I trip over roots, oh, what a ground!

A raccoon thief swipes my trail mix,
His belly jiggles, it's quite the fix.
I chase him down, in playful pursuit,
He looks back, makes me hoot.

Among the ferns, we play all day,
Creating mischief in every way.
The sun dips low, laughter just stays,
In this glade, where silliness plays.

Memory's Thread in the Pine-Scented Air

Pine needles crackle, the sound of cheer,
Bumblebees buzz like they own the sphere.
I dance with shadows, a jig with glee,
While trees shake branches, what a spree!

A flight of squirrels, they plot and scheme,
While I chase them, caught in a dream.
They scatter nuts, I trip and fall,
Nature laughs, what a funny call!

With acorns rolling, I make a mess,
My hat's a perch for a bird's express.
A fox pops out, with a sly little grin,
"Oh, are you lost? Come join in!"

In these scents, sweet memories flow,
With every laugh, the moments grow.
Through pine-scented paths, I gleefully roam,
In this merry space, I feel at home.

Moonlit Glades and Shadowed Trails

Under the moon, we softly creep,
Chasing shadows, losing sleep.
A rabbit jumps, a twig it breaks,
I trip and fall—oh, what a mistake!

Glowworms giggle, dancing around,
While I search for my lost shoe found.
The owls hoot in a merry cheer,
'Look at the human, full of fear!'

A raccoon peers with curious eyes,
Planning a heist beneath starry skies.
I whisper, 'Hey, that's my snack!'
It grins and scuttles back with a clack!

With every rustle, my heart takes flight,
Thinking it's a ghost in the night.
Turns out it's just a crafty squirrel,
Chasing his tail, in dizzy whirl.

A Tapestry of Leaves

Crunching leaves beneath my feet,
I try to dance, it's quite a feat.
But down I go, a muddy slide,
Frog jumps over, laughs with pride.

Colors burst in shades so bright,
I try to taste a pretty sight.
But sticky sap from a friendly tree,
Isn't quite what I thought it'd be!

A squirrel offers me a nut,
With a wink, it gives a strut.
I nod and smile, what a charade,
As it scampers off, I feel betrayed!

Twigs entangle in my hair,
A fashion statement, I do declare!
Critters gather for a good laugh,
While I play tree, what a gaffe!

The Call of the Wildflowers

Wildflowers bloom in hues so bold,
Bees parade like they're covered in gold.
I wave to them, a friendly spree,
But all they want is my cup of tea!

Daisies poke fun, 'Where's your flair?'
As I tumble down without a care.
Butterflies giggle, fluttering by,
'You call that a dance? Oh my, oh my!'

A bumblebee buzzes, 'Get in line!'
'But I'm not a flower, surely I shine?'
It rolls its eyes, snickers with glee,
'You're a funny one, come dance with me!'

I twirl and swirl, but grass holds tight,
Down I go again—oh, what a sight!
The wildflowers cheer, a riotous crew,
Their laughter echoes—this was fun too!

Breaths of the Ancient Grove

In the grove where the ancients sigh,
I stumbled on roots, oh my, oh my!
Whispers of trees like an old-time bard,
'That's not how you walk!' Oh, how I'm scarred!

Mossy carpets, a cushioned fall,
Land soft on my rear, I heed the call.
A crow caws, 'Take notes from the wise!'
As I dance like a goof, beneath their eyes.

I argue with mushrooms, 'Don't look at me!'
They shrug and sprout like they're carefree.
'You think you're sly under those leaves?'
I swear they're gossiping with the trees!

Time warps here, humor in the air,
Even the shadows play with flair.
As I exit, leaves join the laugh,
The ancient grove knows how to craft!

Lost in the Green Sanctuary

I took a path less traveled, oh dear,
But ended up face to face with a deer.
It glanced at me with a puzzled stare,
I waved like a fool, but it didn't care.

The trees were whispering secrets, I swear,
Their branches flailing, without a care.
I dodged a branch, thought I could be spry,
Only to trip on a root, oh my!

A squirrel laughed from high in a tree,
In my fashionably mismatched spree.
I swear they're plotting, those critters so spry,
A furry brigade with a chance to spy!

So here I dangle in nature's embrace,
Lost, but with joy on my goofy face.
With every twist and turn, I find delight,
Next time, I'll stick to paths, just maybe tonight!

A Dance of Dappled Light

In glimmers of sun, the shadows play,
A spotlight on insects that boogie away.
I joined in the fun, a bizarre little jig,
Only to step on a poor, squished twig.

The ferns waved at me, like they knew a dance,
Inviting me closer for a clumsy prance.
I twirled and I whirled, made the butterflies flee,
They whispered, "Oh dear, look at that silly bee!"

A mushroom applauded, all puffed and proud,
While I tripped over roots in front of a crowd.
With every misstep, laughter echoed loud,
In the dance of the light, I felt supremely wowed!

So let's toast to blunders in this shimmering show,
For nature's funny moments are often aglow.
I'll keep on grooving in this vibrant patch,
Just promise to catch me if I hit a snag!

Footsteps on Leaf-Litter

Crunch, crunch, goes the leaves beneath my feet,
A symphony of sounds, oh, isn't that neat?
But suddenly, it's a slip and a slide,
I pondered my choices, then went for a ride!

Each footstep is tricky, a ponderous game,
A dance with the ground, oh, such a shame!
A brick-breaker rock or a sneaky grass snake,
I swerved like a pro, no accident to make!

A rabbit watched, with its ears standing tall,
Munching on clover, it giggled at my fall.
"Just part of the fun!" I quipped with a grin,
As I brushed off the leaves, trying to win.

With every slip, I embrace the absurd,
Nature's comedy club, it seems so preferred.
And if I keep shuffling, I'll surely discover,
The joy in the stumble like an eager lover.

The Art of Quiet Discovery

In silence I tiptoe, I sneak and I peer,
The bushes are stirring, but I'm filled with cheer.
A rustle and shuffle, what could it be?
A rabbit, a hedgehog, or something more free?

I crouch down low for a closer look,
A toad jumps right past, oh what a nook!
It croaks with such passion, it thinks it can sing,
But honestly, it sounds more like a spring.

Leaves flutter down, whispers in my ear,
The trees gossip lightly, full of good cheer.
I blink at a mushroom and think, "What a chap!
I could use a hat for my curious nap!"

Yet still, I wander, with mischief in mind,
Serendipity sparks, I'm a giggling find.
The art of soft steps leads to laughter's embrace,
I dance with delight in this marvelous space!

Ferny Veils and Twisted Vines

In the midst of tangled fronds,
A squirrel wears a hat of ponds.
With acorns tucked beneath each arm,
He struts around with silly charm.

A rabbit hops in clumsy spins,
While giggling leaves fall from the bins.
A fox does somersaults with glee,
While wondering where his lunch could be.

The mushrooms dance in polka dots,
As all the critters share their thoughts.
With every wiggle, twist, and twirl,
The ferns say, "Hey, give us a whirl!"

Among the vines, they hunt for fun,
Training hard to be the number one.
A chorus formed in the happy green,
"Let's make a show, a real mean scene!"

Twilight's Forest Ballet

As twilight dims, the critters cheer,
A ballet starts, they gather near.
With tiny feet and floppy ears,
They leap and twirl to wild frontiers.

The mouse does pirouettes, oh my!
While fireflies light up the sky.
A raccoon tries a grand jeté,
And tumbles down, as dancers sway.

The owls hoot in appreciation,
While crickets play a wild sensation.
In moonlit glades, the laughter swells,
As starlit stories weave their spells.

So join the show, don't miss your chance,
With glowing bugs, we're in a trance.
Beneath the boughs where shadows play,
A night of giggles leads the way!

The Life Beneath the Underbrush

Beneath the leaves so thick and bright,
The ants are planning their next flight.
They march in lines both straight and wide,
While snails just watch from inside their ride.

A worm thinks he's a little train,
Chugging through the dirt with no disdain.
The bugs play hide and seek all day,
And tease the toads who try to play.

A ladybug dons a flashy coat,
While crickets tune their tiny note.
With each small laugh, they blend and blend,
From dawn till dusk, they're never penned.

The world below is full of jest,
With froggy leaps and little quests.
So take a peek, and you will see,
The giggles hum beneath the tree!

A Journey to the Heart of Nature

Let's pack a snack and venture forth,
To find the humor of the north.
With giggling streams and chattering leaves,
Adventure waits in twirling weaves.

The deer wear shades; they think it's cool,
While frogs conduct from a mossy stool.
With every hop and silly prance,
They invite us to join their dance.

The trees may whisper ancient tales,
While mushrooms try to fashion sails.
In this grand play of leaf and bark,
We'll find the joy hidden in the dark.

So follow me through twists and bends,
Where every laugh can make amends.
Tomorrow's paths are bright and fair,
In nature's heart, we love to share!

Beneath the Veil of the Old Oak

A squirrel in a top hat, quite dapper and spry,
Strikes poses with acorns, oh my, oh my!
He juggles them expertly, a marvelous sight,
While the crows just caw, plotting mischief in flight.

A rabbit with glasses reads books on a log,
Critiques all the poems of a nearby frog.
"Your rhyme is quite off, and the meter's a mess!"
But the frog just croaks back, "I'm a sound hippie, yes!"

A fox in bright sneakers does laps 'round the tree,
He's training, it seems, for a race with a bee.
But when he gets startled, he trips on a root,
And lands in the bushes, what a muddled hoot!

Beneath the grand branches, they gather and play,
An acorn debate on the best nutty way.
As twilight approaches, they dance and they prance,
In a hilarious show, not a single mischance!

A Haven Among the Hollies

In a thicket of hollies, the squirrels debate,
Who's got the most shiny acorn-shaped plate?
With opinions as loud as the leaves in the breeze,
"Mine lights up at night!" says one, "How's that for tease?"

A hedgehog named Harry brings snacks to the crew,
He offers up berries, both red and some blue.
But when he trips backward, his snacks fly away,
And everyone giggles, "Let's eat while we play!"

A pair of young owls hoot jokes at the sun,
They tell tales of mishaps while having some fun.
One hoots about lunchtime, too late for a snack,
With laughter and glee, they all gather in a pack!

With nibbles and giggles, they come to a close,
Under branches that sway like a dance of their clothes.
"Next time!" they all cheer, with a wink and a grin,
"I'll bring dessert, or at least muffins to win!"

Reverie in the Woodland Depths

In a patch of bright ferns, the critters convene,
For a game of charades, but it's truly obscene.
The badger tries dancing—a most awkward sight,
While the others just howl at his terrible plight.

A cautious young mouse, with a penchant for pranks,
Releases a squirrel from his chain of shanks.
The squirrel goes reeling and bumps into trees,
And the laughter erupts like a warm summer breeze.

A tortoise who's wise, with a plot up his sleeve,
Declares, "Let's play rock-paper-scissors, believe!"
But they all start to bicker about what's the best,
Thus forgetting the game, joined in merriment's quest.

As twilight does gather, they share all the tales,
Of friendships and laughter that never fails.
Each moment a treasure, they dance with delight,
In reverie, they linger 'til the falling night.

The Rustle of the Wild

A chipmunk in stripes with a hat loud and bold,
Declares to the forest, "I've secrets untold!"
But when he reveals them, it's all just a jest,
And the owls hoot loudly, "Oh, give it a rest!"

A turtle named Timmy won a «slowest» race,
He's crowned as the champion, a proud little space.
Yet every time someone mentions his speed,
He smiles and replies, "I devour with greed!"

The butterflies flutter, in costumes so grand,
They organize parties on mushroom land.
But when the winds blow, they scatter and flee,
Squealing with laughter, "It's a feast for the bee!"

They end with a jabber, a wild celebration,
As fireflies twinkle, a grand illumination.
In the rustle of wild, where whimsy holds sway,
They cherish their moments, come bliss or dismay!

In the Realm of the Relaxed Foliage

Beneath the boughs where sunlight gleams,
A squirrel rehearses acorn dreams.
A chipmunk juggles, what a sight!
While birds debate who's boldest in flight.

The frogs declare it's party time,
With croaking beats, they start to rhyme.
The leaves just shake in laughter's thrill,
As everyone joins, against their will!

A breeze flies in, with whispers loud,
Spreading the tales through leafy crowd.
"Did you see that?" a twiggy voice asks,
As branches giggle, shedding their masks.

So here's to the joy in every nook,
Where nature plays and no one looks.
With critters jesting, and laughter's tone,
This leafy realm feels like home.

Fluid Patterns of Forest Life

In the thicket where shadows play,
A rabbit prances, what a display!
Each leap turns into a tiny mistake,
Landing in puddles—oh, for goodness' sake!

A hedgehog shuffles, slow and round,
"Is this the dance? I've lost my sound!"
So mossy critters join in too,
With wobbly steps, creating a zoo.

The wise old owl rolls its big eyes,
"Why dance so silly under the skies?"
But giggles erupt, not a whisper of fear,
As caterpillars sway with beer mugs near!

And thus they swirl in nature's jest,
With every misstep, they feel so blessed.
In patterns of fun, they lose their strife,
These quirky critters, oh what a life!

Conversations with the Wind

The wind blows softly, a curious tease,
"Have you heard the news from the tall oak trees?"
A rustle of branches, a giggly reply,
"Only what's whispered when squirrels fly by!"

The grass joins in with a ticklish hum,
"Who needs radar? We know when they come!"
A wise old fern adds, "Don't rush, don't fret,
I've seen it all; there's fun in the wet!"

Then butterflies flit, with colors so bright,
"Let's plan a party under moonlight!"
The wind gives a whoosh, "I'll bring the tunes,
What's better than laughs 'neath the glowing moons?"

So, chatter continues, a lighthearted breeze,
Where whispers abound among the tall trees.
With tales of hilarity swirling around,
In these fun dialogues, pure joy can be found!

Swirl of Autumn's Farewell

As autumn dances, leaves twirl down,
A comical sight in rust and brown.
Each leaf that falls strikes a goofy pose,
Like it's taking part in a fashion show!

A squirrel chases, with frantic delight,
"Catch me if you can!" it shouts in flight.
The acorns tumble, rolling away,
"Can someone help? We're not here to play!"

The wind chortles, having a ball,
While pumpkins chuckle, "We're part of it all!"
"Why so serious?" they tease with cheer,
"In the swirl of fun, we lose all fear!"

So autumn's farewell, with giggles galore,
Wraps up the season; there's laughter in store.
With every blow, a chuckle rings true,
As nature giggles, we all join too.

There, Where the Wild Things Grow

Amidst the trees, I meet a hare,
He wears a hat and doesn't care.
He dances round, a funny sight,
As squirrels join in, what sheer delight.

The mushrooms giggle at my feet,
With polka dots, a silly treat.
A bottle fly just flew my way,
He buzzed and laughed, then flew away.

The trees, they whisper all their jokes,
As owls roll eyes like clever folks.
A woodpecker taps, I take a bow,
And hope they laugh, they're laughing now!

So let us frolic, skip and play,
In this green world where oddballs stay.
With every stomp and joyful cheer,
The wild things grow and bring good cheer!

Chasing Light Through the Glades

I skip and hop, I chase the sun,
Through glades where shadows twist for fun.
A fox wears shades, looks oh so cool,
He winks at me—what a fool's duel!

The beams break forth like godly spears,
While I stumble through and face my fears.
A raccoon giggles from a tree,
"Hey, quick! Come now, and dance with me!"

With every step, the flowers laugh,
Some even take a little bath.
The sunlight flickers, plays its game,
And every step feels like a frame.

So let the light lead on my quest,
Through glades where laughter is the best.
In sunlit realms, we'll skip and slide,
With all of nature as our guide!

Moods of the Shifting Seasons

In springtime's blooms, the insects hum,
I spot a frog, he's looking glum.
He frowns and croaks a woeful tune,
While butterflies dance, they're over the moon.

Summer arrives with sun on the beat,
I trip on roots, oh, what a feat!
A hedgehog chuckles, rolls away,
"Can't keep up? Let's nap the day!"

Autumn's leaves let out a shout,
They swirl and twirl, with no doubt.
A rabbit sneezes, oh dear me!
The leaves all giggle, wild and free.

When winter comes with snowflakes bright,
I'm bundled up, oh what a sight!
But snowmen wink and start to sway,
As snowballs fly, it's time to play!

Nature's Embrace in Quietude

In tranquil nooks, a squirrel prances,
While daisies stretch, they take their chances.
A turtle tours with tiny strides,
While crickets chirp and offer rides.

The air is thick with jests abound,
As frogs don caps and croak profound.
A shy wildflower hides in green,
Whispers of jokes, it feels serene.

The brook bubbles, shares its lore,
Of clumsy goats who make a score.
With every splash, some fish will tease,
"Join our splish-splash, it's sure to please!"

In quietude, the forest beams,
With giggles wrapped in sunlit dreams.
And in this embrace, I always find,
A spark of laughter, sweet and kind!

Tapestry of Twigs and Twine

Through the thicket, I stumble and trip,
A squirrel chortles, doing a flip.
A rabbit, bemused, gives me a stare,
As I tangle my feet in a snare of despair.

The trees giggle softly, swaying along,
A chorus of critters singing their song.
I declare I'm the poet of nature's fine stage,
But my hat's on a branch—oh, is that a sage?

With twigs in my hair, I just can't deny,
The forest has secrets, oh my oh my!
I weave threads of laughter, I twist and I twine,
In this tapestry tangled, I've lost track of time.

So if you should wander, take heed and beware,
Nature's a joker, with whimsy to share.
Amongst all the twigs, and the tickling vine,
Don't forget the delight in this journey of mine!

The Canopy Keeper's Tale

High in the branches, a keeper does dwell,
With a cap made of leaves—oh, how swell!
He guards all the secrets of creatures below,
While performing a dance that's rather low blow.

With acorns for buttons and berries for shoes,
He twirls through the air, singing silly blues.
A parrot nearby mocks each step he takes,
As the keeper just laughs, raising bogeyman stakes.

There's magic in mischief, he winks with a grin,
As raccoons steal snacks from the pockets within.
His stories of laughter echo through the pines,
While woodpeckers tap out their own little lines.

He chuckles and shrieks, "Let's play hide and seek!"
But a fox gives him side-eye, "You're far too peak!"
Yet embracing the chaos, he spins in delight,
Under the canopy, all seems just right!

Beneath the Boughs of Belonging

Beneath the grand oaks, I lay with a sigh,
As bees buzz around like they're saying hi.
A raccoon approaches with a glint and a wink,
"Don't worry, dear friend, we won't let you sink!"

With leaves as my pillow and grass for a bed,
I ponder the whispers the mushrooms have said.
A snail spills his guts; he's quite the small talker,
While squirrels debate who is the best walker.

My heart is a sponge, soaking up all this charm,
While a hedgehog rolls by, devoid of alarm.
"Join us for tea!" says the owl from above,
In the heart of the forest, there's plenty of love.

So here in the jumble of laughter and cheer,
Amongst all these creatures, I feel I belong here.
A band of misfits beneath leafy throng,
In this whimsical land, we merrily throng!

A Trail of Echoing Footfalls

Following footprints that dance in the mud,
A bunch of wet squirrels plotting for fun.
A bear steals my sandwich with unkindly glee,
As I shout, "Hey buddy, save some for me!"

The crunch of the leaves keeps a beat with my shoes,
The trees are my audience, with nothing to lose.
I stumble on roots, oh, what a big mess,
The critters all laugh; I'm their main source of stress.

With giggles and grins, I weave down the path,
While frogs leap around, spurring fits of my wrath.
A chipmunk joins in, proclaiming with pride,
"We'll be your cheer squad as you take this wild ride!"

So onward I go, amidst chuckles and cheers,
Collecting the tales of my woodland queers.
For each echoing footfall brings stories anew,
In this journey of laughter, how I wish you could too!

Whispers Among the Trees

A squirrel in shades, wearing a tie,
Tells me a joke as the birds fly by.
'Why did the acorn cross the road?' it said,
'To grow up strong, not to end up dead!'

The leaves are gossiping, rustling with flair,
As I try to dance like I haven't a care.
Owls hoot with laughter, oh what a sight,
I'll join their party, it promises delight!

Beneath a big mushroom, a raccoon does prance,
He's shaking his booty, inviting the dance.
I can't help but giggle, it's quite a scene,
When a fungus throws raves, who knows what it means!

As shadows grow long, the fun's not a bore,
With trees as my pals, who could ask for more?
In this forest of laughter, let's shimmy and sway,
With critters and giggles to brighten the day!

The Hidden Pathways

Down twisted trails, I wander and roam,
With gnomes in the bushes, calling me home.
'Have you seen our garden? It's quite the delight,'
They chuckle and chortle, in leafy twilight.

A rabbit in glasses reads poetry loud,
Reciting fine verses, all for the crowd.
'I wrote this for carrots!' he waves with a grin,
While a hedgehog throws confetti, getting us in!

As I turn the next corner, I trip on a snail,
Who says, 'Take it easy, I'm slow but prevail!'
In a chorus of chuckles, the paths come alive,
Where laughter's the treasure we all strive to find.

With every step forward, I meet a new friend,
In this wacky wild maze, the fun doesn't end.
On hidden pathways where silliness thrives,
I'll dance with the creatures, oh how joy derives!

Echoes of the Forest

In the thickets, I spy a parade of ants,
Dressed up in tuxedos, they waltz and prance.
'Join us for tea!' they chirp with glee,
While a bear claps along, it's a comical spree!

The echoing laughter of branches so bold,
Tells stories of mischief and legends retold.
'Why did the tree wear a trunk for a hat?'
'It wanted to branch out, imagine that!'

A frog with a crown croaks riddles anew,
'What's green and gets thinner the more that you chew?'
The animals giggle, they slap their furry knees,
In this forest of fun, we're joking with ease.

As shadows stretch long, the moon plays a tune,
A dance party erupts, beneath stars and the moon.
With echoes of laughter, we twirl and we spin,
In this grove of delight, where the fun never ends!

Secrets Beneath the Canopy

Beneath the tall branches, secrets take flight,
A squirrel plays peek-a-boo, oh what a sight!
'The acorns have secrets, they won't tell a soul,'
He winks with a smile, 'Come join in the role!'

In shadows of ferns, a parrot squawks loud,
'The trees had a party—what a raucous crowd!'
They swung from the branches, like monkeys in cheer,
With laughter and giggles, oh how we revere!

A fox in a scarf spins tales of delight,
Of hiding and seeking beneath the moonlight.
'You think we play games but we're brilliant at bluff,'
'Come join our escapades, if you think you're tough!'

As whispers erupt, the night takes its cue,
With secrets revealed, there's much to construe.
In this canopy, joy is the key,
With laughter and stories to set our hearts free!

Flickers of Light in the Thicket

In the thicket I dance, oh what a sight,
A squirrel in a tutu, feeling quite bright.
The fireflies giggle, their glow like a tease,
While frogs in top hats croak songs with great ease.

The bushes whisper gossip, branches do sway,
A raccoon with a sandwich steals lunch in broad day.
The owls wear glasses, they study the stars,
While bunnies debate who's the best at hop-hops.

The laughter of chipmunks fills up the air,
As hedgehogs play poker, with no signs of care.
A woodpecker's drumming is quite the funky beat,
While all of the daisies just wiggle their feet.

So join in the frolic, let worries take flight,
In the land of the leafy, where all is just right.
With giggles and grins, we twirl and we spin,
Chasing shadows and dreams, let the fun begin!

Legends of the Leafy Realm

In the leafy realm, tales are truly grand,
Where squirrels wear capes and take on a stand.
The ants make a fortress of crumbs and of cheese,
Building towers while buzzing like bees.

A wise old badger wrote books of advice,
Said, "Never eat mushrooms, they're not very nice!"
The ferns nod in agreement, flapping green fronds,
While rabbits in sunglasses play dueling wands.

At dusk, the fireflies throw a bright dance,
While hedgehogs do limbo, just taking a chance.
The raccoons form bands, strumming sticks with delight,
As the moon starts to glow, it's a magical night.

So gather your pals, hear the stories unfold,
Of mischief and magic, and creatures bold.
In this leafy haven, where laughter does reign,
The legends are wacky and never quite plain!

Veils of Mist and Mystery

Through the mist, there's a rustle, a giggle, a shush,
As the mischievous fog brings a whimsical hush.
The shadows peek out, with eyes big and round,
While the mushrooms wear crowns on the mossy ground.

A gopher in slippers prances about,
While raccoons play charades, there's no room for doubt.
The owls tell bad jokes from branches so high,
As fireflies snicker, their laughter nearby.

A ladybug's party is set on a leaf,
With cupcakes of petals, oh what a relief!
The spiders bring tinsel, each thread is a dream,
While the wind tells a tale of a faraway stream.

So wander with humor, through shadows and light,
In this misty kingdom where everything's right.
Each twist brings surprise, each corner a grin,
For in playful adventures, you'll always win!

Starlit Trails of the Timbers

Under starlit trails, the creatures convene,
A fox with a map tries to find where he's been.
The owls throw a party; they've set up a show,
While hedgehogs in pajamas steal popcorn to go.

The trees tell the tales, with whispers so sage,
Of deer on the runway, who're setting the stage.
A badger in boots models clothes made of bark,
While fireflies flash like they're lighting the park.

The nocturnal jam session gets louder and bolder,
As raccoons trade tips on their summer-time smolder.
Each critter's a star, under moon's silver glow,
In a woodland so funny, just letting them flow.

So dance through the night, in this magical spree,
On starlit trails woven with giggles and glee.
With friends by your side, let the shenanigans start,
In a wonderland where you'll never grow apart!

Ephemeral Moments in the Grove

In the clearing, a squirrel grins,
Chasing shadows and making spins.
A deer mocks with a little leap,
While a rabbit counts its sleep.

Chirping birds join in the race,
Poking fun at the turtle's pace.
They laugh as it slowly crawls,
While nature answers, 'That's how it brawls!'

Leaves drop, as if to say,
'We're just a part of the play!'
But in a twirl, a breeze will tease,
Spinning everyone with ease.

Ephemeral moments, oh what fun,
In this grove where laughter's spun.
With critters dancing, it's quite a show,
In joyous rhythm, delight will flow.

The Silence of Snow-Blanketed Trails

Snowflakes tumble like clowns in the air,
Blanketing trails with frosty flair.
A fox trips over his own furry feet,
While laughter echoes, oh so sweet.

Trees wear coats of shimmering white,
As rabbits hop and give a fright.
With snowballs thrown in playful glee,
Winter's pranksters reign so free.

Footprints lead to a snowman's face,
Dressed in branches, quite the case.
He winks at passers, oh what a tease,
As the sun shines down with gentle ease.

In silence, the snowflakes giggle and fall,
Creating a canvas that wraps us all.
So bundle up, let the fun prevail,
Through wintry laughter on soft, crisp trail.

Heartbeat of the Hidden Retreat

Amidst the trees, a secret hum,
A chipmunk sings, oh what a strum!
With acorns bouncing like round little drums,
Nature's rhythm, it surely comes.

A rabbit hops, twirls around,
While squirrels gather in a merry mound.
The leaves rustle, they join the song,
With every note, they can't go wrong.

Down by the stream, frogs take a seat,
Croaking tunes that are quite a feat.
Their chorus rises in gentle delight,
Echoing heartbeats through day and night.

In this retreat, where laughter plays,
And nature dances in silly ways.
Write it down, let it be told,
The heartbeat of joy never grows old.

The Green Glow of Dawn's Arrival

With morning breath, the forest wakes,
As sunlight skips on little lakes.
A raccoon yawns, stretching wide,
While the owl smirks, feeling pride.

The dew drops giggle on blades of grass,
As the sun peers in, a golden mass.
Flowers bloom with a colorful jig,
While the frogs clap, oh so big!

Squirrels argue, who gets the first nut?
Round and round, they spin and strut.
Their antics spark the greening tune,
As the daylight chases away the moon.

In this dawn, where laughter swells,
Every whisper, a tale that tells.
Embrace the glow, let the fun ignite,
For nature's mischief makes everything bright.

Tales of the Treetops

Up in the trees, where squirrels just play,
A branch wobbles slowly, oh what a sway!
A robin sings loudly, in tunes quite absurd,
While a raccoon rolls by, with a hiccuping blurb.

The owls all gossip, in whispers so sly,
About a lost acorn that thought it could fly.
The woodpecker chuckles, and taps with a beat,
As the branches all shimmy, in rhythm so neat.

A feisty chipmunk, with nuts in his cheeks,
Mocks all the forest with clever little tweaks.
While the leaves shake their heads, on the gossipers' spree,
A squirrel's got snacks, will he share? Oh, we'll see!

So come take a peek at this wacky retreat,
Where the laughter of nature can't ever be beat!
From branches to laughter, there's always a show,
In the land of the tops, where the funny winds blow.

The Magic of the Understory

Down where the ferns sway and mushrooms turn bright,
The critters have parties all day and all night.
A fox brings the snacks, in his clever disguise,
While a grumpy old toad just rolls his big eyes.

Ants march in line with a drum made of twigs,
They dance with the beetles and tease all the pigs.
A spunky old badger joins in on the fun,
With jokes about thistles, the laughter won't run.

The mushrooms are dancing in spots of great flair,
While snails glide on in with their snazzy slow air.
The moonlight is giggling, the stars wink with glee,
As the critters all shout, "More snacks! We agree!"

So if you feel down, take a trip to this place,
Where the low leaves are joking with style and with grace.

In the shade, there's a magic, where funny things grow,
Join in the laughter, it's quite the great show!

A Realm of Bark and Berry

In a realm of berries, where giggles abound,
The bushes all wiggle, with laughs all around.
A porcupine chef, with a menu so wily,
Serves up berry pies, and smiles quite shyly.

The brambles hold secrets, of jams and of fun,
Where the beat of the forest is never undone.
A turtle spins tales, so slow and so grand,
While the raspberries grin and lend him a hand.

The deer prance about, with capers and leaps,
While the blackbird juggles, and nobody sleeps.
Under boughs of oak, the laughter unfurls,
As the critters declare, "It's our berry world!"

So step in the shadows, where chuckles delight,
In the realm of the berry, where fun takes flight.
With juicy good humor and friendship so bright,
Join the laughter parade, it's a pure delight!

The Artisan of the Wild

In a patch of tall grass, where crafts come alive,
An artisan's magic makes critters all thrive.
With twigs he's a sculptor, with leaves he does paint,
Crafting silly masks, of a fox and a saint.

The bunnies all giggle, adorned in new wear,
While the tortoise struts by with an artistic flair.
A butterfly tumbles through works of pure grace,
Making masterpieces in a colorful space.

The owl comes to critique, with spectacles grand,
"Too much purple, dear squirrel! You ought to expand!"
The squirrel just shrugs, with a flick of his tail,
Creating new wonders without fear to fail.

So come join the fun, where the wild has a heart,
In the realm of creation, it's all just a start.
With laughter and curiosity lighting the way,
Be the artisan too, in this playful ballet!

Journey through the Mossy Glade

In a glade where mosses lay,
I tripped on roots that led astray.
The squirrels giggled, held their sides,
As I danced with a bunch of guides.

The mushrooms wink as I pass by,
With tops so round, they surely lie.
"Watch your step!" the toadstools croak,
While the trees chuckle at my joke.

A bunny hops in quite a hurry,
With all my laughter, it's a flurry.
He stops and snickers, shakes his ears,
'Is this a circus, or just your peers?'

Through the glade, I grin and prance,
With every step, I break my stance.
The playful spirits join my spree,
In laughter's realm, we all are free.

Breath of the Wildflower Breeze

The flowers wiggle in the breeze,
In colors bold that tease with ease.
A dandelion blows a kiss,
To bumblebee, in bliss and fizz.

A daffodil with silly cheer,
Dances close to where I veer.
"Watch out for bees!" I squeal with glee,
But they just buzz, all wild and free.

A tulip's hat goes tumbling by,
It lands upon a butterfly.
They twirl together, oh what fun,
While I chase shadows, blocking sun.

Oh wildflowers, in your jest,
You fill my heart; I'm truly blessed.
Among your laughs, I find my way,
In every petal's bright display.

Twilight Among the Ferns

As twilight creeps in soft and slow,
The ferns begin their evening show.
With long, green arms that sway and bend,
They whisper secrets, 'round the bend.'

A raccoon drags a heavy sack,
Of marshmallows for a midnight snack.
The ferns all giggle, what a sight,
As he fumbles under moonlight.

Crickets chirp in a lively tune,
The frogs join in; it's quite a croon.
Each fern is swaying with the beat,
Right in rhythm, they tap their feet.

In this twilight, fun's our refrain,
With nature's laughter, none in vain.
Among the ferns, for giggles and cheer,
Every night feels like a dear.

The Call of the Hidden Grove

In a grove where shadows play,
I heard a giggle, come what may.
A wise old owl with glasses near,
Said, "You'll need more than just good cheer!"

The rabbits plot a cozy game,
With carrots served, but not the same.
A painter's feast, a palette bright,
Where colors clash and take to flight.

A fox arrives with stories grand,
Of trickster tales from distant land.
The grove erupts in roars of glee,
As each one tries to out-joke me.

In this hidden place, we dwell,
With laughter ringing like a bell.
In each small corner, joy's alive,
The hidden grove will always thrive.

The Path Less Traveled

I took a stroll down a path less bright,
Where mushrooms wore hats, and birds took flight.
A squirrel stole my sandwich, oh what a thief,
I laughed and I cried, but mostly disbelief.

A deer joined the dance, with two left feet,
The rabbits all giggled, it's quite the treat.
Nature's a circus, with pranks and glee,
My picnic's now ruined, but I can't help but see.

So I wandered along, and what did I find?
A hedgehog performing, in a tux quite refined.
He bowed with a flourish, the leaves took a spin,
While I, just a guest, soaked it all in.

At last, I returned with a smile on my face,
For every mishap, there's joy to embrace.
This path less traveled has its own charm,
With laughter and magic, it keeps us from harm.

The Sighs of Swaying Grass

Oh, the grass was so green, it started to hum,
It sang me a tune, but I looked rather dumb.
For it swayed to the rhythm of a breeze so light,
Like a concert of whispers, oh what a sight!

A beetle tapped toes, quite skilled with his dance,
While ants clapped along, giving life a chance.
I joined in the jig, though my moves were quite lame,
The grass rolled its eyes, but it played the game!

Then a worm piped up, "Hey, don't step here!"
"Your foot's like a boulder, more like a spear!"
But I leapt and I twirled, with flair and some cheer,
Laughing with nature, with nothing to fear.

The grass sighed with joy, it's a funny old place,
Where laughter and green share a comfy embrace.
We'll dance through the hours, as the sun starts to pass,
In the silly symphony of the swaying grass.

A Harmonious Chorus of Crickets

At dusk, the crickets begin their grand show,
With chirps and with trills, they steal the whole glow.
I clapped to the rhythm, thought I held a good tune,
But my voice shattered silence, like a cow with a swoon.

A cricket rolled over, quite loud and quite proud,
Said, "You're out of sync, let's clear up this crowd!"
With charms and with tricks, they formed a new band,
Playing tunes so wild, it was truly unplanned.

The frogs joined in, with their croaks and their leaps,
While I brought my laughter, as my joy spills and sweeps.

They looked quite bemused, these tiny green stars,
As I wiggled my feet, like I'd danced with a car.

So there in the night, chaos reigned in delight,
A harmony formed, by the moon's gentle light.
With crickets and frogs, it was all quite absurd,
For laughter's the language that needs no word.

Nature's Tapestry of Life and Death

In the forest's embrace, I stumbled on fate,
A raccoon had feasted, it was quite the slate.
With crumbs on his chin, he laughed with delight,
While I gazed in shock at this curious sight.

The flowers were giggling, to see such a scene,
While shadows of owls winked, being quite mean.
"Oh nature!" I sighed, "You're both funny and raw!"
As I watched chomping critters, it was hard to withdraw.

Then a fox pranced by, with a hat on his head,
Claiming he'd eat the raccoon instead.
But they shared a good laugh, a feast for the soul,
While I scratched my head, "Is this the goal?"

Life and death waltzed, with mischief and flair,
A dance of great humor, quite free of despair.
In nature's own theater, we play our small part,
With laughter entwined, it's a curious art.

Dance with the Dappled Sun

Frolicking light through leaves does play,
A squirrel twirls, what a funny display!
Sunbeams tickle the grass at noon,
Even the mushrooms dance to the tune.

Beneath the branches, shadows prance,
Laughter spills as creatures dance.
The fox in a top hat, quite the sight,
Winks at the rabbit, who hops in delight.

Gift of the Gnarled Roots

Twisted roots like fingers stretch wide,
They tickle toes as we choose to glide.
A hedgehog giggles at the sight of my fall,
Rubbing his belly, he's having a ball.

The old tree grumbles, 'What's that sound?'
A bear in a tutu, prancing around.
Nature's oddities make us chuckle and shout,
Who knew the forest could be this sprout?

Promises of Renewal in the Thicket

Budded blooms whisper silly jokes,
Even the toads join in, playing with folks.
A caterpillar fumbles, tries to look brave,
As he slips on the dew, face-first in the wave.

The rabbits hold court, debating with flair,
Who wears the best coat? No one will dare!
With blooms all around, it's a lively affair,
Nature's quirks leave us laughing with care.

Treading Softly on Nature's Carpet

Step lightly, my friend, it's a pastel delight,
The ladybugs march, all dressed up in bright.
A snail's on a mission, what's his great plan?
To race with a worm? They're best of a clan!

Across the soft moss, we stroll with a grin,
When a chipmunk shouts, 'Let the games begin!'
Fungi giggle, as paths twist and turn,
In this merry chaos, there's so much to learn!

Fables of the Forest Floor

In the shade where mushrooms sway,
A squirrel lost his nuts today.
He searched high and he searched low,
But all he found was mistletoe.

A hedgehog danced with glee and style,
While beetles watched and cheered awhile.
'You call that dancing?' one bug cried,
'With those prickles, how can you glide?'

A rabbit tripped and fell in mud,
His fur was brown, his grace a dud.
He hopped back up, with pride and flair,
Squeaking, 'Mud masks are all the rare!'

The trees chuckled, leaves a-flitter,
As rabbits laughed at all the critters.
In this place, where wonders grow,
The fables flow, just like a show.

The Stillness of Wandering

Amidst the pines, a fox does prance,
He thinks he's suave, but lacks a chance.
He strikes a pose, like he's a star,
But trips and falls, not very far.

A raccoon with a flair for theft,
Dodged the traps that others left.
He grabbed a snack, so sly and light,
But missed the sign that said, 'Take flight!'

While birds above sang notes of cheer,
The fox lay sprawled, his face in beer.
'Why do I try?' he moaned in jest,
When all he wanted was a nap, not zest!

Yet in the dawn, they rise anew,
For silliness is what they do.
In quiet woods, such tales are spun,
Where wandering is always fun!

Enchanted by the Evergreen

Under boughs of emerald bright,
A gopher tried to climb a kite.
He waved so high, felt so alive,
Till wind blew hard and took a dive.

A wise old owl hooted in glee,
'See the antics?' he said to a bee.
The bee just buzzed with tiny grins,
'He's as clumsy as my friend who spins!'

A deer wearing a purple hat,
Strolled by the gopher, how about that?
'You'd look great in fashion, my friend,
Just don't tumble, or it's the end!'

As laughter echoed through the glade,
All creatures watched the little charade.
In the evergreen, truth be told,
Funny tales are worth their gold.

Musings Along the Mossy Path

On a mossy path with twists and bends,
Where laughter echoes and fun extended,
A turtle thought he'd race a hare,
And lost the race, but won the stare.

A snail slid by with glitter flair,
'What's the rush? Just stop and stare!'
But turtles pondered slow and wise,
While hares were busy chasing flies.

A chipmunk tried to juggle seeds,
But spat them out just like he'd sneezed.
'Next time I'll stick to nuts and leaves,
Juggling's not my style; it grieves!'

So together they'd laugh and play in glee,
In a patch where everyone agrees.
For on this path, forever spry,
Silly musings float and fly.

Shadows of the Ancient Trees

There once was a squirrel in a cap,
Who thought he could take a long nap.
He snored so loud, oh dear me,
The crickets all fled, on a wild spree.

The rabbits all gathered in fright,
To see the old squirrel's strange plight.
They giggled and laughed 'neath the oak,
At the sight of him dreaming, what a joke!

A fox wandered in, full of grace,
And tripped on a root—what a case!
He rolled down a hill, all in a spin,
Landing right next to the snoring kin.

With laughter, the forest awoke,
While the squirrel just snored, what a joke!
He missed all the fun, quite a pity,
But the woods held a party, oh so witty!

Echoes in the Underbrush

In the thicket, a badger had plans,
To start a band, with four furry fans.
They played in a circle, quite a ditty,
Until they found their rhythm, oh so gritty.

A hedgehog with maracas so bright,
Joined in the fun, oh what a sight!
He shook and he rattled to their sweet tune,
But spiky and prickly, he cleared the room.

A wily old raccoon with a flute,
Joined in the chorus, sounding quite cute.
But he played it wrong, oh what a mess,
Now every note sounded like stress!

They laughed till they cried, oh what a show,
In the underbrush, where cheer would grow.
With echoes of joy that rang all day,
The forest band continued their play!

Secrets of the Sylvan Path

A turtle once wandered, quite slow,
Searching for treasures, or so he'd show.
He bumped into mushrooms, all shiny and bright,
Thinking they'd lead to a sweet surprise tonight.

A wily old owl watched from her tree,
Snickered and hooted, 'What could that be?
A path full of secrets, oh what a find!
But that turtle's so slow, he's lost in his mind.'

The path twisted round, like a silly old snake,
And the turtle just smiled, "For goodness' sake!"
He found a warm pond, with lilies galore,
Plopping right in, a big splash and more!

The owl rolled her eyes, what a sight!
A turtle so happy, oh what delight!
With secrets and giggles, the forest did cheer,
For the turtle found treasure quite close and near!

Dance of the Sunlight Through Leaves

In a glade where the sunlight took flight,
A bee held a disco, oh what a sight!
Under the beams, he buzzed with great flair,
With moves so slick, in the warm summer air.

A ladybug tripped, oh dear, what a spill,
She spun like a ballerina, against her will.
But up she got, spreading laughter anew,
As the whole forest joined in the cue.

The worms wiggled wildly, in grooves oh-so-fine,
While a caterpillar slid on the green vine.
They rolled and they tumbled, all full of cheer,
Everyone danced, as the sun disappeared.

With shadows retreating, the night came alive,
Creatures content, in the glow they would thrive.
What a party they had, all under the trees,
In the dance of the sunlight, happiness frees!

Sway of the Branches in the Breeze

The branches sway, they dance and tease,
A squirrel's acrobatics, oh what a breeze!
With leaves that giggle in sun's warm glare,
They whisper secrets that float in the air.

A raccoon in a top hat, quite the charmer,
Tripping over twigs, an accidental farmer!
He thinks he's suave, he struts with pride,
But in muddy puddles, he must now hide.

Birds are gossiping from a nearby tree,
About Mr. Fox and his odd fashion spree.
With polka-dot socks and a bright blue tie,
He's the talk of the woods, oh my, oh my!

As twilight sets in, they all gather 'round,
To gossip and giggle at the nightly sound.
The critters laugh under the moon's soft glow,
In a comedy club where the wild things flow.

Beacons of Light in the Gloom

Fireflies twinkle like tiny stars,
Guiding the lost, no need for cars.
A glow-worm's disco, a fateful night,
Where dancing shadows give quite a fright.

A raccoon with a lantern leads the way,
While owls ooze wisdom, chattily sway.
"Whooo are you?" they ask with a sly little grin,
While a fox rolls his eyes, "Let the games begin!"

Mice hold a party beneath the tall ferns,
With cheese and gossip, everyone learns.
The hedgehog DJ spins tunes on repeat,
"Don't stop the dance, feel the rhythm, feel the beat!"

In the dark, they find humor, not a trace of dread,
Chasing their tails, laughter widespread.
Light-hearted mischief as night drifts away,
Leaving behind giggles to brighten the day.

The Colorful Canopy of Life

In hues of green with splashes so bright,
The trees wear outfits that capture the light.
A parrot in neon, much too loud,
Complains of the way the oak feels so proud.

Frogs in top hats, croaking a tune,
While butterflies dance, oh what a boon!
The petals are singing, the grass plays along,
Nature's own orchestra, a cacophonic song.

Bumblebees buzz with a wiggly cheer,
Stirring up laughter as they draw near.
"Oh look at that clumsy chap!" they proclaim,
As he tumbles and fumbles in a feathery game.

With the sky painted pink, the sun starts to fade,
The antics continue, no plans have been made.
Together they giggle till stars fill the air,
Life's vibrant tapestry, a whimsical affair.

The Secrets of Twisting Roots

Beneath the soil, where shadows reside,
The gnarled roots giggle, their secrets they hide.
A worm in a top hat, oh what a sight,
Sipping on dew, feeling quite light.

They debate and they bicker, the spiders all win,
With tales of the critters that make their skin spin.
"Oh, did you hear about that clumsy old bear?"
They titter and tattle with spider-thread care.

Grass snakes in sunglasses, feeling all cool,
Sliding and slithering, breaking the rule.
They glide through the roots, and with joyous delight,
Conspire to prank every passing wood sprite.

As night wraps its cloak and the moon shines bright,
The roots crack up, in pure, merry fright.
Each secret they share adds to their glee,
In the depths of the earth, it's a party, you see!

In the Company of Tall Sentinels

In the shade of trees so grand,
I whispered jokes to the forest band.
The owls rolled eyes, the squirrels did laugh,
As I tripped over roots, what a silly gaffe!

Raccoons on branches, giving me guff,
Claimed my peanut stash, oh, how tough!
A squirrel with swagger, a feathered cap,
Challenged me to a nutty mishap!

Moonlight danced through leaves so bright,
I missed the branch, what a sight!
The trees sighed softly, a chuckling crowd,
As I tangled my limbs, feeling quite proud!

But patch up my pride, I won't concede,
I'll twirl with glee, in forest's lead!
For laughter echoes where shadows creep,
In the company of sentinels who never sleep.

Reveries in the Silent Grove

In a grove so still, with whispers low,
I danced with shadows, putting on a show.
The mice took bets, as I twirled and spun,
An awkward ballet, just for fun!

The mushrooms chuckled, a psychedelic sight,
"Don't take a misstep, or take off in flight!"
A deer passed by, with a knowing grin,
See how these antics make heads spin!

I stumbled upon one bushy tree,
In a comical blow, it got back at me!
A branch to the nose, quite the dismay,
"Hey, watch it, buddy!" I had to say.

The air was thick with humor and cheer,
Amongst all the giggles, I held no fear.
In a silent grove where the moments bloom,
Laughter is the echo, dispelling the gloom.

Whispers of the Forest Floor

Stumbling through brambles, I laughed like a fool,
The grass tickled toes, what a merry duel!
"Step lightly!" chirped a wise old crow,
As I juggled acorns, putting on a show!

Under leaves rustling, secrets took flight,
A hedgehog chuckled, what a curious sight!
"Careful there, partner, you're losing your way!"
I just winked back, full of playful sway.

The roots played tricks, I tried to outsmart,
But the forest had plans, a real work of art!
I tumbled and rolled, in a comical spin,
The daisies all cackled, let the fun begin!

With whispers that danced on the soft forest floor,
I embraced the chaos, wanting more and more!
Amongst giggling leaves that swayed to the roar,
Life's sweetest moments, a whimsical score.

Beneath the Canopy's Embrace

Beneath leafy arches that shelter and sway,
I pranced like a kid, come what may!
I chased after shadows, but who could foresee,
That a mischievous squirrel was faster than me!

In the pockets of green, laughter took flight,
As I twirled like a leaf, in pure delight.
I stumbled on daisies, kicked mud in the air,
While butterflies giggled, without a care.

Beneath the grand trees that swayed from the breeze,
I made friends with toadstools, with humor to please.
A wink from a badger, a nod from a hare,
"Get up, my friend! Take a breath of fresh air!"

So here in this haven, where joy is the game,
I dance with the shadows, never the same.
Each step holds laughter, each turn brings delight,
Beneath the canopy's embrace, everything's bright!

www.ingramcontent.com/pod-product-compliance
Lightning Source LLC
Chambersburg PA
CBHW071854160426
43209CB00003B/546